Thank You Jesus

Luke 17:11–19

(Jesus Heals 10 Men with Leprosy)

Mary Manz Simon

Illustrated by Dennis Jones

SAINT LOUIS

In memory of Dr. Velma E. Schmidt
Revelation 2:10

Books by Mary Manz Simon

Hear Me Read Level 1

What Next? CPH
Drip Drop, CPH
Jibber Jabber, CPH
Hide the Baby, CPH
Toot! Toot! CPH
Bing! CPH
Whoops! CPH
Send a Baby, CPH
A Silent Night, CPH
Follow That Star, CPH
Row the Boat, CPH
Rumble, Rumble, CPH
Who Will Help? CPH
Sit Down, CPH
Come to Jesus, CPH
Too Tall, Too Small, CPH
Hurry, Hurry! CPH
Where Is Jesus? CPH

Hear Me Read Level 2

The No-Go King, CPH
Hurray for the Lord's Army! CPH
The Hide-and-Seek Prince, CPH
Daniel and the Tattletales, CPH
The First Christmas, CPH
Through the Roof, CPH
A Walk on the Waves, CPH
Thank You, Jesus, CPH

God's Children Pray, CPH
My First Diary, CPH
52 Ways to Raise Happy, Loving Kids
    Thomas Nelson Publishing

Little Visits on the Go, CPH
Little Visits for Toddlers, CPH
Little Visits with Jesus, CPH
Little Visits Every Day, CPH

Copyright © 1994 Concordia Publishing House
3558 S. Jefferson Avenue, St. Louis, MO 63118-3968
Manufactured in the United States of America

Library of Congress Cataloging in Publication Data

Simon, Mary Manz, 1948–
    Thank you, Jesus: Luke 17:11–19: Jesus heals ten men with leprosy / Mary Manz Simon; illustrated by Dennis Jones.
        p.   cm.   — (Hear me read. Level 2)
    ISBN 0-570-04762-5
    1. Healing of the ten lepers (Miracle)—Juvenile literature. 2. Bible stories, English—N.T. Luke. [1. Healing of the ten lepers (Miracle) 2. Jesus Christ—Miracles. 3. Bible stories—N.T.) I. Jones, Dennis, ill. II. Title. III. Title: Jesus heals ten men with loprosy. IV. Series: Simon, Mary Manz, 1948– Hear me read. Level 2.
BT367.H47S55   1994
226.7'09505—dc20   93-36192

3   4   5   6   7   8   9   10   03   02   01   00   99   98   97   96

"Good morning," said a man.
"Good morning," said his wife.
She looked at his hand.
She shook her head.

"Look," said the man's wife.
"Something is wrong.
Something is very wrong.
Something is wrong with your skin."

The man looked at his skin.
"Oh, no!" he said.
"Something is very wrong."

"I must go to the priests," the man said.

The man ran through the town.
He ran to the priests.

The priests looked at the man.
They looked at his skin.
They shook their heads.
Something was very wrong.

"Go," said a priest.
"You have a sickness.
You must live outside the town."

"You cannot live with your family,"
said another priest.
"You cannot pray with your family.
You cannot go fishing with
your friends."

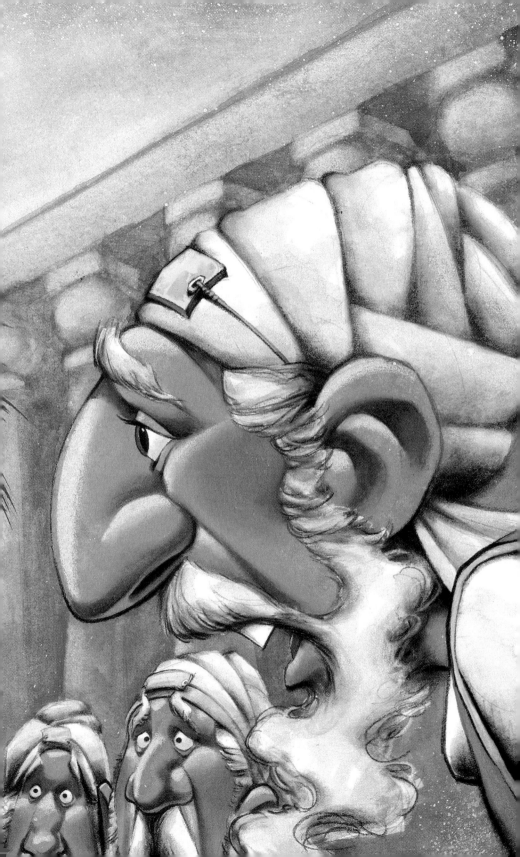

Another priest said, "Other people
have the same sickness.
Live with them outside of town.
Live there until we see
that you are healed."

The priest said, "Go.
Go now.
Come back if you think
you are healed."

The man walked slowly
out of town.

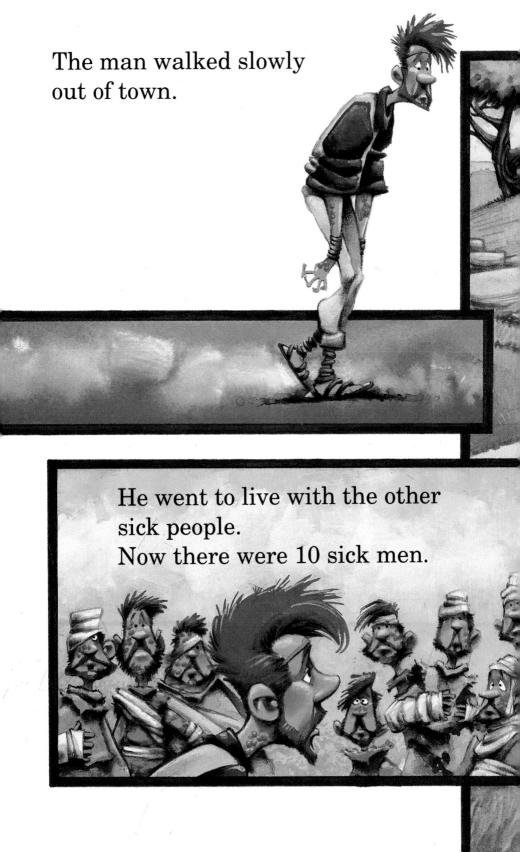

He went to live with the other
sick people.
Now there were 10 sick men.

The man's family wanted
to see him.
He could call to his family.
He could shout, "Hello."
But he could not go near his family.

The man could wave to his friends.
He could yell, "How is the fishing?"
But he could not go fishing with his
friends.

The man could pray.
He could pray outside the town.
But he could not pray with his family.

One day the 10 sick men heard that
Jesus was coming.
"Jesus is coming!" they shouted.

They knew about Jesus.
Jesus taught people about God's love.
He taught people to pray.
He taught people about God's love by
telling stories.

Jesus healed sick people.
He made them well.
Now Jesus was coming here!

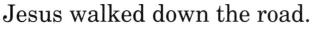

Jesus walked down the road.
The 10 men saw Him.
They waved to Jesus.
They called to Jesus.

"Jesus! Jesus, please help us!"

Jesus looked up.
He saw the 10 men.
He saw them waving to Him.

"Jesus! Jesus, please help us!"
the sick men called.

"Go," called Jesus.
"Go show yourselves to the priests.
Go now."

The 10 sick men started to walk
down the road.
They would do what Jesus said.
They would go to the priests.

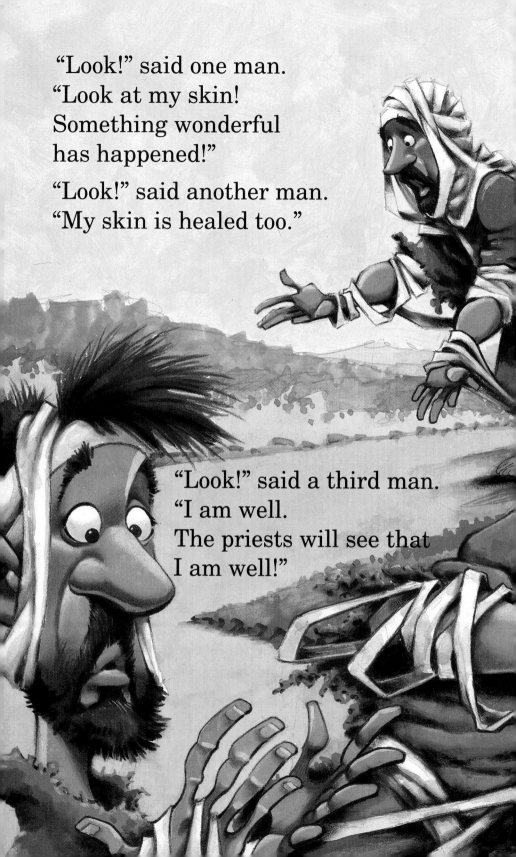

"Look!" said one man.
"Look at my skin!
Something wonderful
has happened!"

"Look!" said another man.
"My skin is healed too."

"Look!" said a third man.
"I am well.
The priests will see that
I am well!"

"We must hurry," said another man.
"We must hurry to see the priests."

Jesus had made all 10 men well!
Nine of the men quickly ran home.

But one man stopped.
He turned around.
He ran back to Jesus.

This man fell at Jesus' feet.
"Jesus, thank You," he said.
"Thank You, Jesus.
You made me well."

Jesus said, "I made 10 sick men well.
But only one came back.
You are the only one who said,
'Thank You.' "

Jesus helped the man get up.
"Go," said Jesus.
"Go now.
Your faith has made you well."